TERRORS OF PARADISE

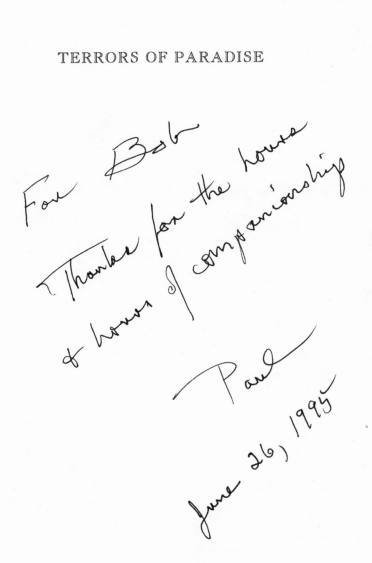

For Bob

Thanks for the hours
& hours of companionship

Paul

June 26, 1995

TERRORS OF PARADISE
By Paul Quenon

Black Moss Press
1995

©Abbey of Gethsemani
Trappist, Ky 40051

Published by Black Moss Press, 2450 Byng Road,
Windsor, Ontario, Canada, N8W 3E8.

Black Moss Books are distributed in Canada and the U.S. by
Firefly Books. All orders should be directed there.
In Canada, they should be sent to:
Firefly Books
250 Sparks Ave., Willowdale, Ontario M2H 2S4 Canada
In the U.S., order should be sent to:
Firefly Books (U.S.) Inc.
P.O. Box 1338
Ellicott Station
Buffalo, New York 14207

CATALOGUING IN PUBLICATION DATA

Quenon, Paul
Terrors of paradise

Poems.
ISBN 0-88753-278-0

1. Title.
PS3567. U32T4 1995   811'.54   C95-900512-

PRINTED IN CANADA

Table of Contents

I Hall of Mirrors

II Tamed By Wildlife

III Songs of Sanctuary

IV *Contained by Angels*

It seemed to be a desert of solitude.
Actually, it was a paradise of delights
— Guerric of Igny
Sermon for the Annunciation.

I Hall of Mirrors

Labyrinth of the Wilderness

There is no getting out of this place.
Life closes in on every side!
Upward is the same sky as
Downward, envelops the same globe
Whereon I've plotted y
Impossible knot.

Outward are mirrors million, reflecting
Inward, where lurks the Minotaur.

The Hall of Terror is the
Palace of Truth
You but kiss the Beast,
The complete compass
Fills with the Royal Image of the
Child of Mercy.

Wild Dogs

Wild dogs on the horizon
Baying in the darkness
Souls of the lost
Wandering, frightened,
Baying out from the midst of
Fading off, returning
In the breeze, lost in my sleep
Crying from by-gone valleys
Beyond reach
Baying on
Forgotten.

No prayer for dark beasts in the wilderness.

Vigil of a Novice 1959

In the darksome air unseen
A night-watch dwells
Forever awake to all that stirs and dies.
Under roof and cover sleep the watchers,
Soon to join the Vigil, soon to be aroused.

Chimes in the tower descend three unsteady steps,
And a hand reaches into the darkened corner
For a bell rope.

Stop your ears
While the pulleys creak
And the screechers preach
As the people sing
"Shame on Nelly in the bell."
At two-fifteen
The sleepers wake
Who hope the rope will break
And resolutions make,
Before they touch the floor,
To daily elevate
Their morning suffering -
O how the bell does ring!

Doors open, footsteps pass
Circulation moves
        through arteries, pipes and cloisters.
A novice's first thoughts are on
The mercy drowned out by the bell
        before he knew it.
"Domine labia mea aperies
        et os mea annunciabit laudem tuam."
"Domine" - Lord
        "labia" - label ?
        "aperies" - apiary, (sure!)
        "Os" - bones.
"Lord open my lid and the bees fly out
        and my bones will announce you loud."

My neighbor's loud
God is loud
Laud be to Deus
all through the day
the daisies praise Deus
in the daisy's own way.

"Frustulum" is for frustration
"Mixt" is for mixed-up
        in confusion in-
            fusion
            in
the deepest form of prayer.

Two slices of bread
        sets it all straight
And a cup of coffee sets me
Off free for
        an hour, free for
        the night, free for
        All, free for
Awful God!

Unquiet Vigil

Stale prayer from
Unreal depths -
Depths I assume are mine -
Relieved by
Real sleep,
Awakens me to my
Real shallows where
Prayer amounts to
Almost nothing
Or less.

Such an infinity where
Almost nothing
Dividing endlessly
Never reaches
Nothing
Wherein are
Real depths
Not mine -

Be kind.
Myself to myself be kind.

Uncle Sam's Silo

Yes, Sonny, your Uncle put this silo on the farm
because he's proud of it and of all this land.
He's holding something in store just in case
the Russians ask for it. What's in there gives
the world food for thought if not for stomachs.
Believe me, my boy, because that silo's so deep
we stand tall. What's waiting inside no weevil
can infest nor rat destroy. When famine comes
no one will rob it, even though it's got the biggest
pay-load you've ever seen. And you can count on it,
once delivered it will bring the biggest kick-back
you could imagine. After that, there'll be no more
famine and hunger, no more sowing, sweating and
harvesting. Everything will be dark and peaceful
as a long winter. No need for sun, there'll be fires
around the horizon where every American city too
gets fed from silos overseas. Then will everybody be
at rest finally, even the cattle and sheep. And if you're
able you'll look at that silo and remember how proud
your Uncle Sam was of you and this land
with all its plenty.

Gethsemani: Almost Paradise

So much beauty at such an hour was all wrong!

Scarcely could the scented garden sense the dread
       I brought into it —

I not knowing whether the beast following me would die

Or whether its teeth and nails would grow longer
       and consume me entirely.

It was driving me apart from my companions, yet
       — such an impossible moment —

I wanted them nearby; happy, confused friends,
       who joked of our sweating wine and seeing angels.

So I buried my face in the dust.

Into that dumb, forgetting earth
       I cried my Father's name.

Would that these stones raised up children of Abraham
       to aid my stifled breath!

From the ground came the prophet's voice:

       "Let him put his mouth to the dust —
       there may yet be hope:
       let him give his cheek to the smiter,
       and be filled with insults."

Up I started to see if the others too had heard.

They must have thought I lay there to sleep —
       already were they unconscious.

And thus I saw our agony had begun.

I wildly shook their sluggish bodies, blindly

      hoping to reverse the slow avalanche
      of things coming apart

      — as if by pressing back, when it first begins
      the whole weight might by one hand be arrested.

Scarcely had I raised a second alarm, "Abba!", when

      my shattering echo betrayed my mistake
      as it ran along the weakened cracks
      of that mighty glacier, which at one sharp cry

      would descend.

Quick, my heart, banish these fatal thoughts!

A small thing before the Father this —
      a chalice that can pass.

And when beneath my quieted breath
      I scarcely uttered:
        "Abba"

I felt a gentle hand above, as if an angel
      inclined to caress.

And looking up I saw there

      Judas

      leaning near to kiss.

Wind Without a Name

In the sullen calm of mid-day darkness,
From the lethal green of a thickened sky,
Across the southern valleys veiled by rain
Comes a sudden wind with no name.

On a high deck I wait, and expect
I-know-not-what,
And cycle lines from a legend written by a monk:

> *"Out of the rains and darkness of the south,*
> *Out of the shadows of the equator*
> *Into which the lightnings have departed*
> *Come fires upon the calm waters of the Pacific".*

A few somber rain-drops betoken serious intent;
The wind grows earnest and brings a torrent,
The torrent brings God-knows-what.
Tree tops in worship bend beyond their capacity.
A smashed chair appears and another on the run.
Across the courtyard, a riff of lumber sounds destruction
And overhead serenely drifts a great sheet of roof,
        ribs and lattice intact —
        a slow ghost-ship sailing on the clouds.

I close the door and
Wreckage slams past the door like a train.
What's a bombing like? I ask
As a hundred feet more of roof
slides into the courtyard.

Insurance assessors, incredulous, had heard nothing of the wind.
Media called it neither cyclone nor hurricane,
Never gave it name, male or female:
A neuter wind was it, with no name.

As the anonymous rain departs
Comes a bus-load of anonymous alcoholics.

By dozens they swarm through the yard among the monks
Clearing debris, the Abbot in the lead with chain saw.

Strangely familiar these men who use first names only,
Like monks who never use their last.
Each hiding ravages of some private storm,
Each confounded by some lonely helplessness.

"Give us a ladder and we'll do it", I hear:
Some experienced roofers in the crowd
Are soon atop the business offices
Replacing corrugation over the computer rooms -
Every electrically recorded name saved by this team of the nameless.
The lectern soaked in church, sounding post of holy names,
Gets sheltered by these the unnamed-may-be-unchurched.
Roof of the library, tomes of the famous
Gets tarped over by these - you might say - unfamous if not infamous
       Rich men, poor men, beggermen, thieves,
       Doctors, lawyers, Indian chiefs,
The rare, the raw, the riff and the raff,
God's motley crew come paddle His raft.
Many are called, the chosen are few,
When you don't have a name,
Well, what can God do?
You pick up a board and haul it away
And think how Jesus redeemed you that way.

Compline over, the monks now retiring,
Ten hungry roofers, work completed,
Stride confidently down the cloister's twilight.

At the darkened end burns a single candle.

> *"I do not recognize the names of the men*
> *who come up out of those fires with diamonds in their hands,*
> *but I look up...and count the incredible mountains."*

Vespers

One after one,

The bells all sink into the shadow
       of the lost hollow.

One after one,

The bells all lost in the hollow

One after one

Sink in the shadow of
       the hollows of the bells

  after one, all sink
       yes, bell after bell
       in the shadow of the hollows

One after one

Shadow after shadow
       in the hollow of the bells

Where're the shadows? where're the bells?
       where's the hollow of the lost?

Bell within bell

One after one,
All in the shadow of the hollow of the bells of the
       bells all the bells...

In the haze of the vaulted forest   rises a bell.

II Tamed By Wildlife

January Eclipse

Because the muted moon
    is sinking behind
    the shadow of earth
It comes alive,
    that pale orb,
    with the warm blush of flesh.

Because the evergreen trees
    stand beneath a coat of ice
    their shoulders slump
    towards earth.

I bend over in the dark and pull on
    heavy winter socks,
which crackle and glow there
    where the thunderstorms of summer
    have gone into hiding
    around the skin of my feet.

Winter Daybreak

Were I not given ears,
how could I hear this silence?
Without eyes, how see
this almost empty sky
with its broken fiction of clouds?

How hear the distant hush
of asphalt under rolling tires,
or see the awesome wings
of haunted clouds?

I thank You for ears
to hear this silence —
the bird that speaks before
I listen, swift sky-mote
falling in the dark and banking
into light, stirring
the orange dawn.

The scratch of my thoughts run
with the bark of the crow
who claims the horizon his,
and leaves this center for
me and all the civilized
freaks he avoids,

where we crowd our ears with
the clank and quarrel of daily
work. For ears

that hear not Your silence, Lord,
O rebuke me;
with the twit-twit of
the titmouse at dawn.

Footprint of God

Farewell, my beloved,
Nothing is lost
Where what is lost
Is nothing.

The imprint the oyster and I
Leave upon the sand
Is a vestige within a vestige.

For all the shorelines of the ocean
Are but sand scraped out
From under God's fingernail.

Swifts Sail

Swifts sail
Over the book bindery
Circle and twist
Down the chimney stack
Like smoke in reverse.

Will they ever come out again?
Has time forever lost its end
And only returns to
Where it began?

Hermits, Hermitages

Hermits, hermitages,
Ages and ages of
        hermitages.
A stupa against the timeless sky,
A shadowy door beneath low branches.

A place where the soul sorrows,
        yes, once a sorrow owns, then turns
        and sees it never again.

Hermits and ages of
        hermitages —
Where do they come from?
Where do they go?

Mild December

Out by night among trees and whispering grasses
I press neck and shoulders to the ground,
Hear the crickets' winter dreams
And feel the sleepless strength of earth —
The rain dry almost as wild grass seed
In the hesitating air.

Do you hear the crickets' winter dream?
It's the same song they sing all summer long.

Elegy for Six Black Kittens

Animals do not despair, the philosopher said,
        they grow sad, but they do not despair.
        Humans despair.

The stray cat had six kittens and all were black.
        Seven black spots on the green grass,
        and a black dog made eight.

The dog strayed off with the summer
        and the kittens disappeared.

The season for strays is gone,
        but black mother cat stays on.

Her bags are full, she bears discomfort.
        They say a cow will reabsorb its milk.
        They say she is making music as she paces about
        looking for the kittens.

All these days the bags remain full,
        the music goes on all these days.
        And the kittens have not come back.

Not despair but sadness, says the philosopher.

Roc Concert Haiku

to Fr. Peter Aikens, died 1986

Facing the sunrise
Roc pens note on window sill
Here in the monk's jakes.

Roc through refect'ry,
No shoes, hole in socks, two cups,
— Monks hurry to None.

That limping specter
Without belt and scapular!
— Roc hunting supper.

Roc Hobbies:
Sunfish, watches, cassettes, cardinals, opossums,
Flat boats, turkeys, parakeets, guitars, blue gill,
Talmud, Jacinta, glue, string, diet pop, turtles,
Bishop Sheen, Mel Bay, rosaries, Sonys, the Little
Flower, bamboo poles, birdseed, tricycles, metal cups,
Nun jokes, gold teeth, holy relics, sandals,
Sunfish.

Elegy for an Old Man Drowned in Our Lake

Who was it?
That old guy who used to walk along the highway.
Always carried a sack to collect beer cans —
They found him in the middle of the lake.
Must have been floating around for two weeks,
        nobody goes there.
He lived all alone. Had a house full of chickens and dogs.
        Kind of a hermit.
He must have been getting water because there were two buckets.
Might of leaned over and fell in —
        Seventy years old.
Always walking along the highway
        and the dogs liked him.
Wore a brown shirt and trousers and had a red wagon sometimes.
        You must have seen him dozens of times.
Drowned in St. Basil's lake.
Some kids found him on a walk but it must have been a long time
        and nobody hardly goes there.
        All by himself.
I can't remember his name again...

Spring Rumpus

Rock and run the wrestler wind
Wakes the resting trees for spring,
Whips the watertower's giant legs,
Brashly hums a hornet hum.

Creak the aging church roof rafters
One by one old knuckles crack the
Sturdy back of pray'n mother.
She don't mind her rampage kids —
Winds young pass over every year.

Robber at my quaking window
Shook my pretty room today,
Snatched her tender breath
— clean away.

Beware, beware! the old wall grumbles,
I'm in no mood to play.

Farmer's Almanac

Sun.   Rain, until the clouds lift. Meteors after 9 p.m.
       Watch the northeast for unexplainable flash.
       This is the day of the whiffle tree.

Mon.   Overcast, no rain. The hens will be restless,
       a good sign the atmosphere is changing.

Tues. Increased humidity aggravates the gout. Grouse
       are migrating south. Follow flight direction
       and plant winter wheat perpendicular to their line of
       flight. Geese and ducks likewise.

Wed.   Narrow bands on the woolyworm forecast a hard
       winter. Don't wear red today, it will bring frailty.
       Last chance to burn the fields until November.

Thurs. Tornados in the midwest, with double-barreled
       funnels. It was on this day that Brian Tucker
       discovered madgewater.

Fri.   Soreness in the knees indicates deficiency of lime.
       If soreness continues, reduce calcium. Westerly winds
       in a rowdy mood. Sunshine, fair. New moon, with
       Saturn standing in Gemini. A cow in labor will
       produce twins. A wife visited on this night will
       produce twins.

Sat.   Conditions normal until mid-afternoon, when
       heavy thunder and hail accompany fire-balls,
       followed by storms of cicadas and snakes in
       great numbers.
       Use Ramon's laxatives. If pain increases,
       consult a physician.

Feud of Monks and the Wee Beasts

Asphalt is spackled white
Where grackles
Concentration bombed
Across the walkway
Between kitchen and library.

Mice are feeding indoors this summer.
Evil days are upon us.

Church-bats
Peppered the floor
At the corner where monks
Bow and turn.
Bad favors for the sacristan.

With rifle in hand
A monk protects his flowers
From the bunnys.

Will nobody tell what started this grievance?

The Short and Miserable Life of a Church Wasp

As if a dragon stepped from the headletter in a psalter
        and flew into the jet age with swept back wings,
Not to terrorize the countryside
        but to search curiously ledges and corners and edges
        of books and choir stalls —
And to tempt apprehensive monks.

Some secure their recollection by letting the marvel fly.
Others take it as a visitation of the devil incarnate
And in a flurry of flailing sleeves and dodging heads
        strike the dragon down and smash him underfoot —
A martyr of the misguided zeal of
        an allegorical confusion.

Saint George pray for us!

15 Poems About the Tree and Me

1. I walk under the tree
      and the tree passes over me.
2. I walk past the tree
      and the tree stands at attention.
3. Around the tree I circle
      and the tree asks no questions.
4. Above, branches; below, roots.
      I stand just about in the middle.
5. Over there the tree, over here me
      an epistemological problem.
6. The tree gets inside me
      so I can get inside the tree.
7. Now, where are the tree and I?
      That's my question, not the tree's.
8. I kick the tree
      and my foot feels abused.
9. All hail, O mighty giant!
      Stay away from writing poems.
10. There really isn't a poet beneath a tree.
      The tree is a poetic fiction.
11. Beware of trees at night,
      and resist glancing at one over your shoulder.
12. The evolutionary tree is completed in me.
      Now begins the etiology of tree.
13. We all have our roots.
      Monkeys the roots, we the leaves.
14. An ancient gash in the tree;
      a harbor for the sickly soul.
15. This obligatory verse about me
      to honor the fifteenth tree.

How The Milky Way Came to Be

After God framed the stars, the heavens were littered
with stardust. East Wind rose and swept all the debris
into the west. But West Wind did not like that, so he blew
all that dust back into the east again. There arose
a mighty conflict of opposing winds, and neither could prevail,
so all that stardust was heaped up between the two winds,
right across the middle of the sky.

So, lest anyone be unhappy about this, God made up a story.
There was a cow who lost her calf. She searched the earth and could
not find him. She searched the waters and no calf was there. Many
days passed when no milk was drained from her udder. When finally
she searched the heavens, milk began to drain from the overloaded
burden of Mother Cow. The calf then smelled the trail and picked
it up, and found his way home.

God called that the Milky Way so we would forget what really
happened, about the terrible battles and the litter left from the
framing of the stars.

III. SONGS OF SANCTUARY

My Silence is the Lord

My silence is the Lord.
I listen, his silence speaks at all times.
When I listen not, my hearing is filled with words
And my tongue takes to rambling.

My resting place is the Lord,
A hideaway on a mountain height.
The lonely seek and find him.

My resting place is the Lord,
A low valley by the runlet.
All humble steps lead there.

"Turn in to my place and sit quietly.
Drink from my stream and my vintage.
Cast off your shoes, discard your hardships
And listen to my evening song:

I seek a heart that is simple,
With the peaceful I spread my tent.
I will wash your feet and dry them,
My silence will be their perfume.
In your quiet steps I will follow,
None will know whence we come, and where we go.
To the world you will be my silence.
In your passing they will hear me.
In your absence I will be present.
Though you die, I Who Live am yours —
I live as yours forever."

Final Vision

In your oneness I am one.
In your eye, the pupil am I:
Not seen except by seeing,
Unheard except by hearing.
What song will be my music?
What utterance my name?

God knowing — such may I be.

Love, loving unto love.

IV. CONTAINED BY ANGELS

The Consecration of a Poet

to my Mother who died October 1983

With a new poem in hand
I swing the door open
And onto my lips sweeps
An insect
— sweet with a sting —
As I walk to the copy machine.

This delight made acute with pain —
Is that the kiss of death, Mother,
Or taste of the words I sing?

Advice For A Solitary

for Donna Herp

She told me to play some, the lady
With eyes bright and arms flailing
Because she was spastic.
"On retreat pray, read, sleep and play."
So play I do. I would anyway.
She knows it is good:

How, is beyond conjecture.
My play is a controlled loss of control.
Does her mind alone
Play, or is it fun in control-
ing what hard - ly can be con t-
rolled? I'm too shy to ask.

Across the open ground I spin and flip —
Or sort of do — with hands on
Earth and my feet
In air, while the rain comes down
And wind, mild wind, takes thought away
And leaves this only care.

Elegy for Brother Pachomius: Guestmaster

Slow shuffler with hang-dog face,
Eyes looking up are marble shines.
Doctor Emeritus of flowers and
       culinary crafts
Turning a corner as if
       the walls move and you alone stay still.

That stocking cap covered a head
       from which nothing of the world was hidden.
In which all things swam in the mild season
       of a gentle vision: the harsh and heartless
       with the true and pleasant.

And so guests came, mothers and uncles, kids and babies,
       birds and dogs, the news, the worries,
       the personal stories.
And were set at ease and made at home
       before they knew how or why.

As the year ends, and the rain falls
       You lay down for a long, long nap —
and warm clouds scurry towards the north.

I go to my room and quietly close the door
       catching a glimpse between here and reality
Of your face, ruddy not grey:

Eyes looking up are happiness shines.

Return of The Old Watertower

On the night breeze comes the ghost of an odd friend,
Once conspicuous for his racket.
The south wind no longer clatters and clanks,
But whistles and falls silent.

Cranky old thing, ugly enough to stop a hurricane -
Proctective idol of the yard buildings!
Straddle-legged and bossy,
Steel-laced right up to the hips.
Holding aloft his own counsels:
We never got them, though our life depended on it,
Until poured into our drinking cups.

Was that a spike on his helmet or crusader's cross?
— a Quixote windmill fending off errant knights.
Sad that there were none among these
Soft-stepping monks.
Occasionally a monkey among them climbed up to his
Shoulder and waved at the audience,
Fixed metals, tightened belts,
And painted a new uniform.

Lonely sentinel, his one neighbor
A church steeple with whom he would
Never reconcile.

On windless days he waited rusty and inert
As Dorothy's tin man,
A bird's nest stuffed in his ear,
The siren horn gone deaf when
The tool building caught fire.
Tons of water held ready and useless
Because the fire truck wouldn't start,
And the alarm system was unplugged.

I awake and hear November winds moving north
Without audible damage. Perhaps they might find the old King Lear
Now wandering stupidly some solitary tundra,
Frozen water bursting the seams of his head,
And icicles sprouting splendidly
From his towering frame.

The New Watertower

to my Abbot, Timothy Kelly, a Canadian

Ocean breeze green,
Serene as a cucumber peeled.
Quiet benefactress skirted about with trees,
Separated becomingly from
Monks and their private affairs.
Not inconspicuous quite, but simply unnoticed;
Discreet as a northerner is likely to be.

It would be lovely to fade into a heaven
The color of your air,
But you never mention heaven,
And the soul is our affair.
Your vertical dimension does
Terminate kind of square.

"See yourself to spiritual drink, child:
Mine's of the practical sort."

Mother of Time

In the middle of night there comes a pause
     when time goes to sleep.
If grace, fortune or some feral instinct
     you should awake
You are nowhere between the time you went to sleep
     and the time you will wake up.
No use asking the clock for time gone to sleep
     and slipped off, leaving nothing
But this empty space where slow and fast
     cannot compete,
Where before and after are unoriginate —
     no more than twins struggling
In the womb of a sleeping mother who is
     you forgotten by yourself.

Three Vignettes

Three monks pass one another
On a cloudy afternoon.
One turns and looks at wood pallets outside the dairy.
Another follows from behind.
A third in stocking cap nods and smiles
The delight of the day.
They go silently in three directions
And eternity does not forget
This place and moment when
Three Trappists pass one another
On a cloudy afternoon.

† † † † † † †

One Ancient of Days
In cloth shoes, scarcely able to lift
One foot in front of another,
Waits for dinner. Dinner is always served
At 12:30, but he waits for dinner every day.
His neighbor arrives with hands full of books,
So with his cane he hooks the stool
And pulls it into place for him.

† † † † † † †

A young monk asks the old
Will you be the next one to die?
He peers up with grey-green eyes:
"O, I've been dead for six years."

46

On the Womb of Angels

I don't know any angels, because I've never met one - or none has gone out of its way to meet me. Perhaps going out is something angels never do, and going in is the only way they go.

Angels must hide inside one another and need no outside at all, for all hide inside God who is invisible. If I ever do meet an angel I will already be inside it. And there I will see all other angels, as though peering through a series of crystal concentric spheres, so perfectly fitted they appear as one.

Angels begin inside one another, containing and contained. An unborn angel is one that is lost until another finds him in herself, where he always was, but never knew himself to be until that other thought herself different.

And so an angel never leaves his womb; his womb-angel is no different from himself but merely not the same. Generator and generated know the other as self.

Two mirrors face to face reflecting in unending series, mirrors within mirrors. With the beginning all were created at once, emerging first as Lucifer and Michael. Lucifer brought the light to Michael and Michael reflected it. Whole and entire that image was taken in, immediate, complete, intuitive: and thus did a third angel emerge.

Thus an angel devours its own womb and emanates as a third which, in turn, becomes its abyss, until all are consumed in one embrace, face within face, each enclosing the whole, the whole for each its place.

Is not an angel a coincidence, a metaphysical coincidence? Only in another does it exist. In truth, an angel does not exist. No. An angel in-sists. Its being is to be not outward but inward, like a hole in a river, the whirlpool disappearing like a black hole in space, too heavy ever to be seen, consuming the light, for light is its food and drink.

One angel decodes another, order within order unending, sameness within samenesses, a proliferation of implicit totalities. So how many angels can dance on the head of a pin? Why, all of them of course, simultaneously!

I don't know any angels, as I say — unless it could be, that is all I have ever known.

I Nocturne

Dry Bliss

Only this half moon now
while this now is not yet eternity.

Only dusty veils rolling over the slow moon
while the All is yet unseen.

A frail trickle of water I hear,
only a shy early cricket
while the unutterable is yet unsounded.

This silence is music unto itself,
but is my rarified purgatory
scarcely mentioned at all in poems,
to the catechism a closed book.

Nobody told me how to get here
or asks how long I will stay.

Strange mercy this dry bliss,
which poets miss, the religious dismiss

for only the poor
so gentle a kiss.

II Nocturne

A tenor dog punctures the dark horizon like a yard light.

Dark vines climb the pale garden wall
    and mass their blackness with fir trees

where nests the cradle moon in deep crystal air
    under the arching foliage of an elm tree.

Frail crickets linger on the threshold of silence.

Out in this cold air, with coffee warm inside,
    a blanket of still air wraps itself around me
    but does not nip.

Water, the constant water, echoes
    round the enclosure walls.

Headlights creep past the wall slots —
    a stranger departs from this quiet nightbed of prayer

and another, alone, arrives.

4:15 a.m.

Once again night.
Not until I quiet once again
to the cricket's song do I know
how many fathoms of noise
I have descended:
each strata humming with some shade,
sullen and territorial,
some stubborn rancor,
some muted deflated desire,
until
at the murky bottom a hole
drops into an open sky
of night air, small insect sound,
and the distant bark of farm dogs.

One House

A starless sky, the ground featureless:

    one same earth where

Rwanda, Haiti, Bosnia

    happen.

Same floor, same ceiling,

    one same

    House of God.

So insufferable a place to sit,

    but sit I do.

The Wayward Moon

The wayward moon
Rumples up a confusion of
Clouds 'round the sky,
Trees rise bare and tall,
A blue spruce surges
In dark waves to a point,
As hills roll under the limpid
Touch of moonlight.

A dog somewhere makes
Distant argument, another
Rebukes, while a third
Yaps and warbles long
As a train down a valley.

But the careless moon
Has no ear for quarrels.
Tomorrow the last shave
Of shadow will fill
And she'll sail round
And clear of the random
Netting, where stars are
Snagged and lost, gems
Scattered in a restless
Bed chamber

All these years I have worked
Towards a certain life,
And now I have it.
Then why rankle so
Over shades of inconsistency?

Tomorrow the moon will
Sail round and clear
As the day of birth
Naked as the eye of Divinity.

III Nocturne

All fallen silent now, not a night creature sounds,

    the stars rising up in chorus

    too immense to be heard,

more ancient than any visible thing.

    Yet the light is as young to itself

as when it first left that star.

My sight is cleansed in its liquid light.

Perhaps the star burnt out aeons ago,

    the light travels so far.

Yet the light pours down

    ever as new, still young

when I am extinguished and long forgotten.